Barista
Coffee

Making the perfect cup of coffee
and delicious cakes to have with it

APPLE

First published in the UK in 2011 by
Apple Press
7 Greenland Street
London NW1 0ND
www.apple-press.com

Computer Typeset in
ITC Avant Garde Gothic
Printed in China

ISBN 978-1-84543-426-7

PUBLISHER: Anthony Carroll

GRAPHIC DESIGNER: Elain Wei Voon Loh

SERIES DESIGNER: Elain Wei Voon Loh

FOOD PHOTOGRAPHY: Paul Nelson, R&R Photostudio (www.rrphotostudio.com.au)

FOOD STYLIST: Lee Blaylock

RECIPE DEVELOPMENT: Michelle Keogh, R&R Test Kitchen, recipes on page 157 and 161
were provided by Tamara Milstein: tamara@tamaraskitchen.com

BARISTA: Mitch Faulkner, Barista Trainer, Retail Food Group Limited

INTRODUCTION: Samantha Carroll

PROOFREADER: Stephen Jones

Special coffee roasting images by ESPRESSOLOGY *Coffee Roasters for Expert Baristas*

The publishers would like to thank the proprietors of TRE ESPRESSO BAR of
459-475 Sydney Road, Brunswick, Victoria for their assistance with photography
of their espresso bar for this book.

Contents

introduction

'Barista' is an Italian word for one who has mastered the espresso machine, and an expert on brewing and mixing espresso beverages.

Coffee is one of the most traded commodities in the world, second only to oil. Coffee is grown in over 50 countries throughout the world, with many of those economies dependent on this great commodity.

In this book we instruct you on how to become a 'coffee artist', through our pages of 'coffee art' instructions, together with some great recipes for coffee cakes and biscuits.

Now you have your own coffee machine you can start to use it like a barista.

The process of preparing and serving espresso-related beverages seems, to the average person, a relatively simple task. However, as you start to use your machine you will find, initially, that the production is anything but simple. In fact, it is a rather complex matter and will require a good deal of practice. Learning to extract café-quality espresso from your machine is like learning to shuffle cards – it takes practice but once the skills are obtained you will never look back.

You will notice that we refer to 'crema' a lot in our instructions. You may innocently ask, what's that?

Crema (or *schiuma* in Italian) is the heart and soul of true espresso flavour. Crema is the creamy, golden brown extraction that develops in the filter holder and settles at the top of your espresso serving. Delicate oils in the espresso grind form colloids (very fine gelatin-like particles with a very slow rate of sedimentation). Crema is evidence that the correct amount of fresh coffee was ground to the proper consistency, and the precise amount of water at the correct temperature was quickly forced under pressure through the fine espresso grind.

The history of coffee

Most people know the mythical tale of how coffee was first discovered. Back in the 9th century, Kaldi, a humble Ethiopian goatherd observed how his goats danced and pranced about after eating the red berries of what we now know as the coffee plant. Amazed by the excitable behavior of his herd, Kaldi collected some of the magical berries and consulted a holy man who cast them into a fire.

The aroma produced by the roasting beans was so intoxicating that they were quickly retrieved, ground up and infused into hot water: history's first cup of hot coffee!

Since then, coffee has been the drink of choice of practitioners of political intrigues, social uprising and creative thought. Just how did the humble cup of coffee come to be ringside at the great shifts in cultural history in the West?

Coffee came to Italy from the Ottoman Empire during its thriving trade with Venice in the middle of the 17th century and the inaugural Venetian coffee house opened its doors in 1645. It took an Italian to establish the first café in Paris where, over mugs of hot coffee, Voltaire, Rousseau and Diderot developed the philosophies that would lead to the French Enlightenment.

Coffee houses soon spread like wildfire across Europe and became a focal point of social interaction. By 1675, England had more than 3,000 coffee houses. Authorities feared that such places encouraged political dissenters to gather, drink coffee and plot against the current monarch. Indeed, coffee drinkers at the oldest coffee house in London were implicated in plots to assassinate William III. Yet it was the same London coffee house that started listing stocks and commodity prices and evolved into the London Stock Exchange. Auctions held in coffee houses during the eighteenth century also laid the groundwork for the great auction houses of Sotheby's and Christie's.

By 1901, the first espresso machine was patented, which forced boiling water and steam through ground coffee and into the cup. Unfortunately, the high heat of the water gave the coffee a burnt flavour, but, by World War II, piston machines replaced steam and kept the water at the optimal temperature. Because a lever was pulled to produce the coffee, it was colloquially called 'pulling a shot'.

By the 1960s, pump-driven machines replaced manual pistons and became standard in espresso bars.

At the same time, coffee bars were becoming venues for counter-cultural performances by beat poets and folk musicians of the like of Bob Dylan and Joan Baez.

Coffee drinking took on an entirely new face in the 1970s and 1980s with the explosion of standardised coffee bar chains into popular franchises. Such bars prided themselves on high-quality beans and superior equipment to produce an excellent standard of coffee.

By the 1990s, consumer espresso machines brought café-quality coffee into the home. Such machines sported a high-voltage pump that generated excellent crema and a wand for steaming and frothing milk, making it possible for consumers to produce a cup of espresso of equal quality to those made by commercial machines.

Creating the Perfect Espresso: The Four Ms

'Espresso' has become the shorthand for 'caffè espresso', the beverage produced by forcing very hot water through finely ground coffee under force. It is this process that creates the elusive crema – the intense, silky layer of orange-brown foam that is the signature of an espresso coffee.

It is said that making the perfect cup of espresso coffee requires the four Ms: Miscela, Macinazione, Macchina and Mano.

MISCELA – THE COFFEE BLEND

Coffee blends can be chosen for a number of reasons: to create a signature blend, to balance the aromatics of different coffee species or to capture the purity of coffee from a particular coffee-growing region.

Arabica or Robusta – what's the difference?

The two most important species of coffee plant used in coffee production are Arabica and Robusta. Originally indigenous to the mountains of Yemen, Arabica accounts for roughly two thirds of the world's coffee production. It is also produced in the southwestern highlands of Ethiopia and southeastern Sudan, throughout Latin America, India and to some extent in Indonesia.

Arabica's preference for higher altitudes has earned it the name 'mountain' coffee, such as the famous Jamaican Blue Mountain coffee which retails for around $200 per kilogram.

Arabica beans produce a complex coffee taste of superior quality to the Robusta, which is why many coffee blends will boast their credentials as '100% Arabica'.

Robusta, from the species *C canephora*, accounts for roughly a third of the coffee produced worldwide. It is cheaper to grow since it thrives at lower altitudes. Robusta is produced in West and Central Africa, Brazil and South-East Asia, particularly Vietnam. It contains more than twice the caffeine content as Arabica beans, making it is more resistant to pests. Robusta tends to produce a brew that is more bitter than Arabica, and imparts an earthy, even musty flavour.

However, before you decide to reject Robusta out of hand, you should know that only the lower grade Robusta winds up as freeze-dried instant coffee, whereas the premium Robusta crop is still used in espresso coffee blends. Coffee shops may use Arabica as their primary bean but, because it is more expensive to grow, a blend containing some Robusta makes the Arabica more affordable.

Many Italian purveyors use 10% Robusta in their blends for its capacity to improve the consistency of crema.

In France, where they enjoy its bitter taste, the ratio of Robusta to Arabica can be as high as 45:55.

It also comes down to personal taste. Most coffee drinkers are used to the taste of Robusta from the supermarket aisle. Therefore you may find you enjoy the bitter edge and body of the Robusta beans to the mellower taste of Arabica.

Coffee roasting

The roasting process forces moisture out of the bean and brings volatile oils to the surface of the bean. The essence of the espresso flavour is in these delicate oils. The darker the roast, the longer the bean has been roasted, and a dark roast can have less caffeine than a lighter roast. As the heat of the roaster forces moisture out of the bean, the bean expands but the weight, because of the extraction of moisture, diminishes.

There is no precise standardized terminology used to describe the coffee roast. Viennese, Italian, French and American are not the origin of the bean, but instead refer to the degree of roasting, and that depends on the standards of the roaster.

Finding the right blends

A good option for experimenting with the best espresso blend for you is to look at those offered by boutique coffee roasters. There are countless purveyors of fine coffee who select choice green beans, which they roast themselves and then combine into a range of different blends. Many of these roasters have an online presence where you can order excellent whole or ground coffee blends directly to your door. Some even offer sample packs for tasting to enable you to choose which blend suits you. Others even allow you to make your own blend of different regional coffees.

Coffee contains 800 different aromatic compounds – anything from hints of chocolate to smoky, cigar-like aftertones – and these boutique roasters have spent years perfecting different blends for a range of tastes, occasions and even health and ethical concerns.

• *Fair Trade Certified*

Much of the world's coffee crop is grown in developing countries. In recent years, it has become possible to support these producers better by purchasing fair trade certified coffee. This means that the coffee is bought directly from the farmers and growers at a fair price, rather than via conventional trade economics that discriminates against the poorest and weakest producers. A fair trade partnership helps to improve local sustainability and quality of life in these impoverished areas by channelling money into important community infrastructure such as schools and hospitals.

• *Rainforest Alliance Certified*

The Rainforest Alliance is an international non-profit organisation dedicated to the conservation of tropical forests that works to conserve biodiversity by transforming land-use and business practices to ensure sustainable livelihoods. Coffee that is Rainforest Alliance Certified (RFA) is derived from farms and forests where water, soil and wildlife habitat are conserved, where workers are treated well, and where families have access to education and health care. So both coffee consumers and the communities where coffee is produced benefit.

- *Organic*

For coffee to be certified organic, it means that no chemicals or pesticides were used in the producing country of origin.

- *Decaffeinated*

The 'hit' that coffee-drinkers perceive they get from a sip of a good cup of coffee is often nothing to do with caffeine, but rather from the intense flavour.

Good decaffeinated coffee can still offer that flavour hit but without the caffeine.

Decaffeination is usually carried out by the Swiss Water method pioneered by the Swiss Water Decaffeinated Coffee Company in the 1930s. Raw green coffee beans are soaked in hot water to release the caffeine and the beans discarded. The remaining water passes through a carbon filter that traps the caffeine but preserves the coffee solids. The resulting extract is used to capture caffeine from new green beans added to it, creating raw beans that are 99.9% caffeine free. The caffeine is lost but not the flavour.

Those simply wanting to reduce their caffeine, not eliminate it entirely, might confine themselves to 100% Arabica beans only since these contain about half the caffeine as Robusta.

MACINAZIONE – GRINDING THE BEANS

As anyone who has ever sniffed freshly ground coffee beans will know, the flavour of the coffee is at its best immediately after the beans are ground.

In fact, the most discerning baristas will only grind beans for espresso directly before using them. Coffee puritans swear that it only takes 30 seconds in the open air for ground beans to become too stale for a good espresso. It is true that ground beans slowly lose their flavour over time, but this can be reduced if the coffee is properly stored.

How to store your coffee?

If you elect to purchase your coffee pre-ground, you need to remember that all coffee is highly perishable. This is especially true of ground coffee, since so much more surface area is exposed to the air which robs its flavour. Because of this, coffee is often vacuum packed, although even this keeps the beans fresh for only a few weeks. Be warned that many pre-packaged imported coffees are already some months old before they reach the supermarket shelves.

It is best, therefore, to grind your coffee beans yourself of buy your coffee fresh each week. Or, if this is not practical, buy the smallest practical quantity you can manage, and store it in an airtight, moisture-proof container in a cool place. A glass or ceramic container with a rubber seal is ideal.

Importantly, do NOT store coffee in the fridge or freezer. When cold coffee is brought out of your fridge into room temperature, a layer of water condenses on its surface which damages the aromatic flavour oils. Like tea, coffee attracts and absorbs foreign odours, so protect your coffee from contamination from other foodstuffs that can affect the flavour.

Which grinder?

We all know there is no contest between ready-ground coffee and the coffee you grind yourself. Also, whole beans keep far longer than ground, so obtaining whole beans and grinding just before brewing is ideal. There are two main varieties of home coffee grinders – blade grinders and burr grinders.

• Blade grinders

These operate like a small home blender by using fast-moving blades to chop the beans. The grind produced by such machines varies from chunks to fine powder. This inconsistent grind is okay for stove-top or drip coffee makers, but not for pump- or piston-driven espresso machines that require a uniformly fine grind. Such grinders also heat the beans, which can tamper with the flavour profile of the coffee.

- *Burr grinders*

Using a burr grinder will give homogenous grinding so the particle size of the coffee is consistent and even, which is especially important for espresso. If the particle size of the coffee is uniform, equal amounts of the coffee's profile will be extracted. However, if the particle size of the coffee varies, some particles will be over-extracted and some will be under-extracted, resulting in poor tasting coffee.

These grinders may be either electric or operated by hand. They contain corrugated steel burrs that rotate to shave the beans. The benefit of such machines is that may be adjusted to achieve different grinds and they also minimise heat production that can affect the flavour of the coffee.

Before investing in a home grinder, consider how much you wish to spend and how much time you are prepared to devote to use and maintenance. Manual burr grinders are cheaper but require some elbow grease to operate. The more expensive the electric machine, the greater degree of grind adjustment available, which is preferable. The correct grind is a vital step in preparing café-quality espresso – this may require a period of trial and error to fine-tune the consistency of the grind to your particular espresso machine. A grinder that does not achieve the exact grind you require for your coffee machine type will be a waste of money.

Some modern electric burr grinders include electronic sensors for precision grinding and a portion-control container that measures out the precise amount of coffee required each time. Certainly the cost of a burr grinder is worth the investment, because whole beans retain their freshness longer than pre-ground coffee, and you can adjust the grind to suit your machine to obtain that perfect cup of espresso coffee.

Like any equipment used to prepare food, grinders require maintenance and cleaning to be kept in optimal condition. There is little point grinding freshly roasted beans in a machine that contains old coffee residue that has turned rancid.

Which grind?

Whether grinding your coffee yourself or buying it pre-ground, ensure the grind is appropriate for your machine:

PLUNGER	: Medium Fine
FILTER/DRIP METHOD	: Fine
ESPRESSO AND STOVETOP	: Very Fine
GREEK AND TURKISH	: Powder

The grind determines how fast the coffee flavour is extracted. Too coarse a grind will produce watery coffee. Too fine a grind will over-extract the coffee and make it bitter.

Also, the grind has to be uniform in order to ensure the best taste. Generally speaking, the faster the brewing method, the finer the grind required.

For your espresso machine, the beans must be ground fine, but not too fine. If the grind is too fine – a powder grind – water cannot flow through the grind even under pressure. A powder grind feels like flour when rubbed between the fingers. A fine grind should feel gritty, like salt.

If the water flows too slowly or not at all, the grind is too fine for your machine. Another variable is the quality of the coffee used and the pressure applied when tamping the coffee in the coffee basket.

A more powerful machine develops greater pressure and therefore takes a finer grind. However, if the grind is too fine, or the coffee tamped too compactly, the water under pressure in the brew head will not be able to flow through the grind and coffee may spurt from around the filter holder.

The proper grind for your particular machine is critical to extracting a crema espresso. You will need to test the fineness of the grind at different indexes on the grinder before determining the optimum grind for your machine.

If you are desperate, you can pulverise the roasted beans using a mortar and pestle, but this generally reduces the bean to the power consistency required for Greek or Turkish coffee and is too fine for espresso.

MACCHINA – THE ESPRESSO MACHINE

Electric, non-pump machines are the highest selling coffee machines for the home market today. These entry-level machines are cheaper than their pump counterparts, but will still produce a serviceable long black. However, non-pump machines rely on steam pressure and so do not provide the 'grunt' for creating café-quality crema, which is the basis for many coffee beverages as well as the prerequisite for producing coffee art in the home.

To bring the café experience into your kitchen, what you need is a piston-lever or pump-driven machine that generates sufficient pump pressure to force hot water through the fine coffee grind.

Espresso machine pressure is measured in atmospheres (ATM) or pounds per square inch (psi). Non-pump machines only generate pressure to an average of 3 ATM or 44 psi. Pump-driven machine, on the other hand, achieve pressures of up to 9–17 ATM or 135–250 psi.

The latest technology in the home espresso machine is the thermoblock system, which replaces the boiler with a thermal block. Because the water is flash-heated by the thermoblock, steam is continuously available for frothing or steaming milk (while there is still water in the reservoir).

If you are wanting to improve your skills as a barista and experiment with coffee art, you require at least a pump-driven or piston-lever machine. However, if ease of operation is more important, there are also automatic machines that complete the whole ritual of coffee making for you, with programs for different coffee types at the click of a button. Espresso machines are also available in combination with ordinary drip model for households who require espresso-drinkers and drip-coffee drinkers to be catered for by a single unit.

MANO – THE SKILLS OF THE BARISTA

As 'mano' is the Italian word for hand, this final M refers to the talents of the barista. 'Barista' is the Italian word for bartender, although it has come to refer specifically to a person skilled in the art of coffee making.

Even if you have purchased a state-of-the-art espresso machine, making coffee still requires practice. The most important thing is to know your equipment, including the grinder and the espresso machine. Be sure to read the manual that comes with the machine. Thankfully, home espresso machines today require less skill, but the espresso maker is still a sophisticated piece of equipment that requires some initial self-training to use. For example, you need to know how to fill your filter basket properly, how to tamp the ground coffee, the best movements required for frothing the milk.

Like all skills, making the perfect espresso requires practice. There is no rewind switch or undo button when making a cup of coffee, so achieving the perfect crema beings with some trial and error. But, don't take it too seriously – learning to become a home barista is part of the fun of owning your machine. With patience, you will eventually learn to pull every shot with the beautiful crema that is the mark of true espresso.

Coffee art

If making coffee is a science – from the roasting and grinding of the beans to the perfect brewing temperature to extract the ultimate coffee flavour – then creating unique images on the coffee surface is the art.

Coffee art or latte art requires a perfect combination of crema and steamed milk foam. The milk is steamed using the wand on the espresso machine until the stainless steel jug feels too hot to touch but not boiling. The resulting froth – sometimes called microfoam – has a smooth, meringue-like texture, unlike the big-bubbled macrofoam that is no good for making coffee art.

The secret to creating the coffee art canvas is the pour. The milk should be poured at a consistent rate into the centre of the espresso so that the milk disappears under the brown layer of crema or is layered on, depending which design you wish to achieve. A teaspoon and other tools are used add final droplets of milk foam, which are then manipulated against the brown base to create interesting designs. You will be amazed at the dizzying array of patterns you can create with a skewer or a teaspoon: from seagulls to hearts to flowers to leaves to lips to smiley faces!

To make great coffee in your coffee machine, always follow the 5 basic steps...

- Empty old coffee grounds thoroughly

- Rinse out old grounds

- Wipe the handle

- Pack the coffee gently

- Tamp with reasonable pressure (not too hard)

Mitch Faulkner

Mitch is a qualified barista. He started out in a café and was trained by an instructor who demanded perfection. Mitch has managed that same café for 4 years. He is also the New South Wales Barista Trainer for RFG Australia looking after 350 stores. Mitch has judged competitions and trained baristas both in Australia and New Zealand. He prides himself on his barista skills and sharing them with others. Mitch won the Australian Barista Championships Coffee In Good Spirits in January 2010 and competed in the World Barista Championships in June 2010, where he obtained a very creditable fourth place.

Free-Poured Patterns

The hardest form of coffee art is 'free pouring'. This is where we get into creating art, such as the heart, rosetta, apple, tulip, sparrow and other designs.

These are created by simply moving the milk jug a certain way when pouring. Don't be disappointed if you cant get these patterns correct immediately as they are hard to do and require a lot of practice. Ultimately you will need to ensure that you are getting perfect shots and perfect milk every time in order to start trying these designs.

Coffee art is only limited by the barista's artistry, skills and imagination.

POURING THE MILK

You should texture the milk whilst the espresso is being brewed.

Start with the tip of your jug on the edge of the cup and pour steadily. Once the cup is about half full, lower the pour close to the crema and the foam should appear.

You should pour the milk as soon as possible. Hold the cup on its ear and slightly at an angle. Start pouring the milk slowly into the crema. You do not want to pour too slowly, this will leave the foam behind in the jug. You also do not want to pour too quickly because this will break the crema apart. Pour slowly in a few spots in the cup to break through the crema.

Start pouring the milk into the back of the cup once the cup seems just more than half full. Now slowly but very steadily move the pitcher from side to side. This is a wrist movement and should be done just slightly. The milk should not swing from side to side in the jug. Keep moving it from side to side in one spot in the cup until you see the foam appearing. If you see distinct white lines forming, you're on the right track. Keep practising and eventually you will be rewarded with your own latte design.

Once you see the foam break through the crema you can start pouring patterns.

Heart

1 Pour slowly in the middle to settle the crema so you can have a base to work with.

2 About halfway through, start tilting the jug forward to release some froth.

3 Continue pouring into the middle and let the white circle form.

4 Near the top of the cup start tilting the jug back upwards and move to the other side of the cup in a scooping motion.

Tulip

1 This one is a lot like the heart but you start and stop to get different layers to create the tulip.

2 Start pouring at one end of the cup and once you get your first blob of froth in the coffee, stop.

3 Move the jug closer to you and start pouring again until you have a smaller blob.

4 Near the top of the cup start tilting the jug back upwards and move to the other side of the cup in a scooping motion.

Rosetta

1 To start with, pour slowly to settle the crema to give you a good base to start. This allows the milk to separate to form the pattern.

2 About halfway through pouring, move the jug from side to side until you see the foam appearing on the surface. Keep moving the jug from side to side until you see curved white lines appear. Now slowly move the jug backwards while still moving it from side to side.

3 Once you have reached the edge of the cup, start tilting the jug back upwards and move back down the centre of the leaves in a scooping motion.

NOTE Quick movements from side to side will create a rosetta with lots of leaves. Slow movements from side to side will create fewer and thicker leaves.

Double Rosetta

1 To start with, pour slowly to settle the crema to give you a good base to start. This allows the milk to separate to form the pattern.

2 About halfway through pouring, move the jug from side to side until you see the foam appearing on the surface. Keep moving the jug from side to side until you see curved white lines appear. Now slowly move the jug along one side of the cup while still moving it from side to side.

3 Once you have reached the edge of the cup, start tilting the jug back upwards and move it back down the centre of the leaves in a scooping motion.

4 Repeat steps 2–4 on the other side of the cup to achieve your other rosetta.

NOTE Quick movements from side to side will create a rosetta with lots of leaves. Slow movements from side to side will create fewer and thicker leaves.

Rosetta with Chocolate Wreaths

1 To start with, pour slowly to settle the crema to give you a good base to start. This allows the milk to separate to form the pattern.

2 About halfway through pouring, move the jug from side to side until you see the foam appearing on the surface. Keep moving the jug from side to side until you see curved white lines appear. Now slowly move the jug backwards while still moving it from side to side.

3 Once you have reached the edge of the cup, start tilting the jug back upwards and move back down the centre of the leaves in a scooping motion.

4 Using your chocolate sauce bottle, draw two zigzags of chocolate either side of the rosetta. Using a clean skewer starting at top of cup, dip in and drag down through the middle of the chocolate zigzags to create your wreaths.

Indian Head

1 Pour a rosetta (see page 32).

2 Use a teaspoon to scoop out some froth and place on the left-hand side of the rosetta.

3 Using a clean skewer, dip into the crema and etch an eye and a mouth.

Heart with Chain of Hearts

1 Pour a heart (see page 30) on one side of the cup.

2 Using a spoon, scoop out some white froth from your jug and place a white dot on the brown base on the other side of the big heart. Repeat this two more times below the first white dot.

3 Using a clean skewer starting at the top white dot, dip your skewer into the crema and drag through the centre of all the white dots.

Etched Patterns

Milk etching is a form of coffee art that is done by using the milk froth to create a contrast on the coffee.

A lot of care should be taken when pouring the milk so as not to destroy the crema. Spoons, toothpicks, the tip of the thermometer or similar utensils may be used to place the froth on the coffee and create the desired pattern. This may take a little more time but always remember it is more important to serve a good tasting hot coffee, so don't try anything too fancy too fast.

Seashell

1 Pour into the centre of espresso to achieve a white circle on top of the coffee. If in your pour you don't achieve a white circle in the middle of the crema, use a spoon to scoop some froth out of the jug and place in the middle of the cup.

2 Dip the handle of a spoon or a skewer into the white circle.

3 Pretend your cup is a clock face. At 12 o'clock at the edge of the cup, dip your skewer or spoon handle into the coffee and drag back to the middle. Repeat this several times, making your way around the cup.

4 Using a clean skewer, start in the middle and draw a swirl from the centre to the edge of the cup.

Flower

1 Pour into the centre of the espresso to achieve a white circle on top of the coffee.

2 Using a skewer, dip into the white circle, then dip your painted skewer into the crema and drag back to the middle using an arc motion.

3 Repeat this several times, making your way around the cup.

Pinwheel

1 To start with, pour slowly to settle the crema to give you a good base to start. This allows the milk to separate to form the pattern.

2 About halfway through pouring, tilt the jug closer to the coffee angled more open so the froth can start separating, leaving you with a white blob on top of the coffee.

3 Using a skewer, dip into the white circle, then dip your painted skewer into the crema and drag back to the middle using an arc motion. The more lines the better definition.

4 Once finished etching the lines, use a clean skewer to dip into some brown crema then dip skewer into line tips around edge of cup. Continue until all lines have a dot at the end.

Sun

1 Pour into the centre of espresso to achieve a white circle on top of the coffee. If in your pour you don't achieve a white circle in the middle of the crema, use a spoon to scoop some froth out of the jug and place in the middle of the cup.

2 Using a skewer, dip the tip into the white edge of the circle and make your way around the whole circle using an 'S' motion.

3 Using a clean skewer, dip into the crema and draw a face in the centre of the white circle.

Seagulls

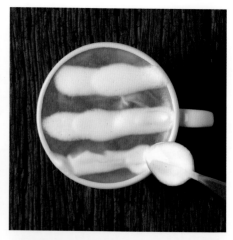

1 Pour your coffee gently to create a brown base on top.

2 Use a spoon to scoop some froth milked out of your jug and create some parallel lines.

3 Place a skewer at the top of the parallel lines. Drag the skewer through the lines, move it about 1cm to the side and drag in the opposite direction. Continue until the cup is full of seagulls.

Chain of Hearts

1 Slowly pour your coffee to get a nice brown base.

2 Using a spoon, scoop out some white froth from your jug and place a white dot on the brown base. Repeat this two more times below the first white dot.

3 Using a clean skewer starting at the top white dot, dip your skewer into the crema and drag through the centre of all the white dots.

Egyptian Evil Eye

1 Pour into the centre of the espresso to achieve a white circle on top of the coffee. If you don't achieve a white circle in the middle of the crema, use a spoon to scoop some froth out of the jug and place in the middle of the cup.

2 Using your skewer, dip deeply into the crema and etch an oval into the white circle. Dip again and draw an eyebrow above the oval. Clean the skewer, dip again into crema and draw a circle inside the oval on the right-hand side. Dip into the crema again and draw a pupil inside of the circle.

3 Using a clean skewer dip into the oval and drag out to create the eye lashes.

Pac Man Eating a Ghost

1 Pour your coffee, trying to achieve a large white circle on the left-hand side of the cup. If you don't achieve the white circle, use a teaspoon to scoop out some froth and place on left-hand side of the coffee cup.

2 Use a teaspoon to scoop out some froth and place a smaller circle next to the large white circle.

3 Using a clean skewer, start outside the large circle and drag into the middle creating a wide mouth. Using a clean skewer, dip into the crema and give the Pac Man an eye.

4 Using a clean skewer on the bottom of the smaller white circles, drag your skewer up a couple of times to create a ghost tail. Clean the skewer off, dip into the crema and etch some eyes on the ghost.

Monkey

1 Pour the coffee slowly to achieve a nice brown base.

2 Use a dessert spoon to scoop out some froth from the jug and place a large white circle at the bottom of the cup. Use a teaspoon to scoop out some froth and place a smaller white circle on top of the larger circle. Use your teaspoon again for the two white blobs for the ears.

3 Using a clean skewer, dip deeply into the crema and etch the line for the mouth with teeth in the large white blob. Clean the skewer off, dip again in the crema and etch the nostrils. Clean the skewer again and etch the eyes in the top white blob.

Panda

1 Pour the coffee slowly to achieve a nice brown base.

2 Use a dessert spoon to scoop out some froth from the jug and place a large white circle in the centre of the cup. Use a teaspoon to scoop out some froth from the jug and place the ears on the edge of the large white blob.

3 Clean the teaspoon off, scoop out some crema and place the eyes and the inner ears.

4 Clean the teaspoon off, scoop out some white froth from the jug and place on top of the brown eyes.

5 Using a clean skewer, dip into the crema then dip into the eyes and etch the mouth.

Bear Face

1 Pour into the centre of the espresso to achieve a white circle on top of the coffee. If in your pour you don't achieve a white circle in the middle of the crema, use a spoon to scoop some froth out of the jug and place in the middle of the cup.

2 Use a teaspoon to scoop out some froth and place the ears on top of the white circle.

3 Using a skewer, dip into the crema and dip into the white ears to create a contrast.

4 Dip again into the crema and etch some eyes and a mouth.

Bunny

1 Pour a heart (see page 30).

2 Use a dessert spoon to scoop out some froth from the jug and place below the heart.

3 Using a clean skewer, dip into the crema and draw the nose, mouth and teeth.

4 Dip your skewer again and etch some eyes.

Shoelace

1 Slowly pour the coffee to get a nice brown base.

2 Use a spoon to scoop out froth from your milk jug and cover half the coffee with it, ensuring you keep an even line in the middle.

3 Using a clean skewer, dip into the white side and drag it into the brown crema. Whilst dragging upwards, move your skewer left and right.

4 Once at the top, drag your skewer down the middle to the bottom of the cup.

Orchid Flower

1 Pour into the centre of the espresso to achieve a white circle on top of the coffee. If in your pour you don't achieve a white circle in the middle of the crema, use a spoon to scoop some froth out of the jug and place in the middle of the cup.

2 Using a thermometer or thick skewer, dip into the white circle then dip into the brown crema at 12 o'clock on the rim of the cup and drag back to the centre. Repeat this at 3 o'clock, 6 o'clock and 9 o'clock.

3 Using a skewer, dip into the centre of the white circle and drag out through the middle of each petal.

4 Dip the skewer into the crema and place a brown dot in the centre of the flower.

Peacock

1 Pour the coffee to leave yourself with a thick white line. You can always cheat and use a spoon to draw the white line. Use your spoon to create a head on top of the thick white line.

2 Using the handle of the spoon, dip into the white froth and etch a white line in the brown crema, dragging back to the white line to create one of the feathers. Repeat this process four times.

3 Using a clean skewer, etch a mouth and an eye.

4 Using a clean skewer, dip into the white froth and then dip into the brown crema above the head to make some white dots – the peacock's head feathers.

5 Using a clean skewer, dip into some brown crema then mark the end of each feather. Use a chocolate powder shaker to dust chocolate over the bottom of the pattern.

Skull and Crossbones

1 Pour into the centre of the espresso to achieve a white circle on top of coffee. If in your pour you don't achieve a white circle in the middle of the crema, use a spoon to scoop some froth out of the jug and place in the middle of the cup.

2 Dip the handle of the spoon into the white froth and etch the bones by dragging back to the centre.

3 Using a clean skewer at the edge of the bones, dip into the crema to make the joints on the bones.

4 Using a clean skewer starting at bottom of the circle, dip into the crema and drag up to create teeth for the skull.

5 Dip the skewer into the crema and etch some eyes.

Swirl Chain of Hearts

1 Slowly pour the coffee to get a nice brown base.

2 Using a spoon, scoop out some white froth from your jug and place a white dot near the centre of the coffee. Repeat this step in a swirl motion until you reach the rim of the cup.

3 Using a clean skewer, start at the white dot nearest the rim of the cup, dip your skewer into the crema and drag through the centre of all the white dots, making your way to the middle.

Galaxy

1 Pour your coffee gently to achieve a nice brown base.

2 Using a spoon, scoop out some froth and place two circles in the coffee.

3 Using a skewer, dip into the white froth and place some random white dots in the coffee.

4 Using a clean skewer, dip in the biggest circle and drag out and then back through the circle, finishing on other side.

5 Using a clean skewer, dip into the centre of the small white dots and drag out into the crema to make the star.

Patterns with Chocolate

The easiest way to make coffee art is to use chocolate syrup to form the design. This is because the finished product is not dependent on the way the coffee is poured. However, it is always good practice to keep as much of the crema on the coffee as possible.

You should never use chocolate milkshake topping for chocolate etching as it destroys the flavour and quality of the finished coffee. The best option is to use a good brand of chocolate powder and mix it with boiling water to form a chocolate paste that sits well on the coffee. Make sure the powder is well mixed and there are no clumps of chocolate powder as a clump may block up the sauce bottle. An even better option is to use espresso shots to mix the chocolate instead of the boiling water – you will find that the resulting flavour is far superior.

Bottles suitable for this application are readily available at your local craft shop or discount variety store.

Note that chocolate etching should only be placed on cappuccinos, hot chocolates and mochas.

CHOCOLATE SAUCE RECIPE

To create your chocolate sauce for your coffees, extract a 30mL espresso shot, add 6 dessert spoons of chocolate powder and mix thoroughly. Your sauce should be nice and thick and easy to work with. If it's too thin and watery, add more chocolate powder. If too thick, add another 30mL shot of espresso.

Chocolate Flower

1 Using a craft bottle filled with chocolate sauce, draw a circle in the centre of the cup. Repeat this process, drawing a circle around the previous one.

2 Pretend your cup is a clock-face. At 12 o'clock at the edge of the cup, dip your skewer or spoon handle into the coffee and drag back to the middle. Repeat this process at 3 o'clock, 6 o'clock and 9 o'clock. Make sure you wipe the chocolate off your skewer each time.

3 Using a clean skewer, dip in the middle and drag out to the edge of the cup to create petals.

Morning Star

1 Pour into the centre of the espresso to achieve a white circle on top of the coffee.

2 Using a chocolate sauce bottle, draw a circle around the white blob. Then draw another bigger chocolate circle around the smaller one.

3 Using a skewer, dip into the crema outside the biggest chocolate circle and pull directly into the centre of the circle and lift out gently. Repeat this three or more times around the white circle.

4 Place a clean skewer deep into the centre and drag out to the edge of the cup midway between two of the existing lines. Repeat three more times around the circle.

Flower with Choc Outline

1 Pour into the centre of the espresso to achieve a white circle on top of the coffee.

2 Using a chocolate sauce bottle, draw a circle around the white blob. Then draw another bigger chocolate circle around the smaller one.

3 Using a skewer, dip into the crema outside the biggest chocolate circle and pull directly into the centre of the circle and lift out gently.

4 Once you have several petals, place a clean skewer deep into the centre of the petals and drag out to the edge of the cup. Repeat with each petal.

Butterfly

1 Pour a heart (see page 30).

2 Using a chocolate sauce bottle, trace the outline of the heart.

3 Using a clean skewer, dip into white froth and etch some antennae at the top of the heart.

4 Using a clean skewer, dip into the crema on one side of heart and drag into the middle. Repeat on other side.

5 Using a clean skewer, dip into crema at bottom of heart and drag up to create the butterfly body.

6 Using a clean skewer, dip into the right top wing and drag out towards the rim of the cup. Repeat on the left top wing.

7 Using a clean skewer, dip into the bottom right wing and drag out to the rim of the cup. Repeat on the left bottom wing. Finally add four dots of chocolate sauce.

Choc Swirls

1 Pour the coffee slowly to achieve a nice brown base.

2 Use a spoon to scoop out some froth from the jug and put a line of white across the middle of the coffee. Repeat again, creating a white cross in your coffee.

3 Using your chocolate sauce bottle, follow the outside outline of the white cross. Then place another chocolate cross in the middle of the white cross.

4 Using a clean skewer, dip deep in the middle of the coffee and start swirling outwards until you reach the rim of the cup.

Sunrise

1 Pour the coffee slowly to achieve a nice brown base.

2 Using a dessert spoon, scoop out some froth from the jug and place in the middle of the coffee. Use a chocolate powder shaker, dust chocolate on half of the coffee, covering half the white circle.

3 Using a clean skewer, dip into the white semi-circle, then pull out and dip in at the far left of the cup rim and drag back to the white circle, creating a ray of sunshine. Repeat several times, making your way right.

Spiderweb

1 Pour your coffee.

2 Using a chocolate bottle, start squeezing chocolate sauce into the middle of the coffee. Make a circular motion with your hand, getting bigger and bigger until you get to the edge of the cup.

3 Using a clean skewer, start at the edge of the cup and drag it into the middle. Repeat this process several times, making your way around the cup. Remember to clean your skewer each time for a nice clean finish.

Christmas Tree

1 Pour your coffee gently to achieve a nice brown base.

2 Using a chocolate sauce bottle, start at bottom of the cup and draw a zig zag, starting big at the bottom but getting smaller as you make your way to the top.

3 Using a clean skewer, dip into the crema at the bottom of the Christmas tree and drag to the top. As a result you will be left with leaves on each side. Using clean skewer, dip in the centre of each leaf and drag out.

4 Using a chocolate sauce bottle, draw a small circle on top of the tree. Using a clean skewer, dip into the centre of the circle and drag out. Repeat a couple of times so it resembles a star.

Lily Ponds

1 Slowly pour your coffee to get a nice brown base.

2 Using a spoon, scoop out some white froth and place 3 circles on the brown base.

3 Using a chocolate sauce bottle, put a chocolate ring around each of the white circles.

4 Using a clean skewer, dip into the white, then pull out and place outside of the chocolate ring and drag back to middle.

5 Repeat this until you have several white lines around each lily.

Boat

1 Pour into the centre of espresso to achieve a white circle on top of the coffee. If in your pour you don't achieve a white circle in the middle of the crema, use a spoon to scoop some froth out of the jug and place in the middle of the cup.

2 Using a chocolate shaker, dust half the coffee.

3 Using a chocolate sauce bottle, follow the outline of the white semi-circle. Next, draw a thick line above the choc powder, then draw a mast and sail.

4 Using a clean skewer, dip into the white circle below the chocolate outline and drag out to the rim of the cup. Repeat this several times moving from left to right. Make sure you wipe your skewer clean each time to ensure a nice clean finish.

Taj Mahal

1 Pour the coffee slowly to achieve a nice brown base. Using a spoon, scoop out some froth from the jug and place a white line across your coffee below the centre. Scoop out some more white froth and place a white circle in the middle and on top of the white line.

2 Using a chocolate sauce bottle, draw three parallel lines across your white line and outline the white circle with chocolate sauce.

3 Using a clean skewer, dip into the crema below the chocolate lines and drag up through the centre of the white circle.

4 Using a clean skewer, dip into where the chocolate circle starts, drag down through the parallel lines and do a u-shape motion dragging back up through the parallel line again and up to the top rim of the cup. Repeat this process on the other side of the coffee.

Coffee with Text

1 Pour your coffee gently to achieve a nice brown base.

2 Use a chocolate shaker and dust half your coffee with chocolate.

3 Using a chocolate sauce bottle, write a name or statement in the coffee.

NOTE I use this when I sometimes make a mistake and write 'sorry' on top of the coffee – customers love it!

Crown

1 Pour into the centre of the espresso to achieve a white circle on top of the coffee. If in your pour you don't achieve a white circle in the middle of the crema, use a spoon to scoop some froth out of the jug and place in the middle of the cup.

2 Using a chocolate sauce bottle, draw your crown around the white circle.

3 Using a skewer, dip in at the edge of the white circle and drag around the edge of the white circle to give your crown a clean finish.

Caterpillar

1 Pour your coffee slowly to achieve a brown base.

2 Using a spoon, scoop out some froth from the jug and place a white line across the cup.

3 Draw a chocolate line along each edge of your white line.

4 Using a skewer, dip in at the start of the chocolate line and drag it back and forth from the white line and brown base, following the chocolate line. Repeat with the other chocolate line.

Choc Sun

1 Pour your coffee slowly to achieve a nice brown base.

2 Using a chocolate sauce bottle, draw a circle in the centre. Draw another circle around the smaller one, then a third circle outside the second.

3 Using a skewer, starting on the outside of the circles, dip into the crema and drag into the centre. Wipe your skewer each time. Repeat this process several times, making your way around the circle.

4 Using a clean skewer, drag out from the centre between each of the existing lines, using a curving motion.

Quick and Simple

1 Pour the coffee and use a spoon to cover it with white froth.

2 Using a chocolate sauce bottle, draw a random continuous circle on the white base. The more circles, the more effective the design.

3 Using a skewer, starting on the outside of the circles, dip into the coffee and drag into the centre. Wipe your skewer each time. Repeat this process several times, making your way around the circle.

NOTE You can use a brown base also but white gives more definition.

Shot Variables

The main variables in a shot of espresso are the size and length. Terminology is standardized, but precise sizes and proportions vary substantially. Cafés generally have a standardized shot (size and length), such as 'triple ristretto', only varying the number of shots in espresso-based drinks such as lattes, but not changing the extraction – changing between a double and a triple require changing the filter basket size, while changing between ristretto, normale, and lungo require changing the grind.

SIZE

The size can be a single, double or triple, which correspond roughly to a 30, 60 or 90mL standard (normale) shot, and use a proportional amount of ground coffee, roughly 7–8, 14–16, and 21–24 grams; correspondingly sized filter baskets are used. The single shot is the traditional shot size, being the maximum that could easily be pulled on a lever machine, while the double is the standard shot today.

Single baskets are sharply tapered or stepped down in diameter to provide comparable depth to the double baskets and, therefore, comparable resistance to water pressure.

In espresso-based drinks, particularly larger milk-based drinks, a drink with three or four shots of espresso will be called a 'triple' or 'quad', respectively, but this does not mean that the shots themselves are triple or quadruple shots.

LENGTH

The length of the shot can be ristretto (restricted), normale/standard (normal) or lungo (long): these correspond to a smaller or larger drink with the same amount of ground coffee and same level of extraction. Proportions vary, and the volume (and low density) of crema make volume-based comparisons difficult (precise measurement uses the mass of the drink), but proportions of 1:1, 1:2 and 1:3–4 are common for ristretto, normale and lungo, corresponding to 30, 60 and 90–120mL) for a double shot. Ristretto is the most commonly used of these terms, and double or triple ristrettos are particularly associated with artisanal espresso.

Ristretto, normale and lungo are not simply the same shot, stopped at different times – this will result in an underextracted shot (if run too short a time) or an overextracted shot (if run too long a time). Rather, the grind is adjusted (finer for ristretto, coarser for lungo) so that the target volume is achieved by the time extraction finishes.

Espresso (Short Black)

Espresso is an Italian name for a coffee beverage. In Italy, the rise of espresso consumption coincided with urbanisation. Espresso bars provided a place to socialise and coffee prices were controlled by local authorities, provided the coffee was consumed standing up. This encouraged the 'stand at the bar' culture.

A true Italian espresso is 30mL of beverage with a thick, golden crema on the surface. True espresso is a complex beverage, combining a special blend of Arabica beans, darkly roasted, finely ground, densely packed and quickly brewed under pressure in individual servings. Properly brewed espresso with crema has a uniquely smooth and creamy bittersweet flavour that captures the full essence of the beans, a distinctive flavour not found in any other type of coffee.

ESPRESSO (SHORT BLACK)

1 Firmly tamp 1 tablespoon of ground coffee to ensure that the water flow is restricted.

2 The pour/extraction should take about 15–20 seconds.

3 Serve in a small 90mL ceramic glass or demitasse cup with a layer of golden crema on top.

NOTE The size of an espresso can be a single or 'solo' (30mL), double or 'doppio' (60mL), or triple or 'triplo' (90mL). The length of the shot can also be varied – ristretto (restricted), normale (normal) or lungo (long).

Long Black

160mL cup, ⅗ hot water, ⅖ espresso (2 shots)

Long black is a style of coffee most commonly found in Australia and New Zealand, but now becoming available in the UK. It's made by pulling a double shot of espresso over hot water (not boiling) – the hot water also comes from the espresso machine.

The order in which a long black is made is important, as reversing it (eg. espresso first, water second) will destroy the crema from the espresso shots. The espresso should be full bodied, with a good crema.

LONG BLACK

1 Place 90mL hot water in a cup.

2 Firmly tamp 2 tablespoons of ground coffee to ensure that the water flow is restricted. Use a twin group head for an even extraction.

3 The pour/extraction should take about 30–35 seconds.

4 Serve in a standard 160mL ceramic or glass cup with a layer of golden caramel crema.

AMERICANO

A similar coffee is the Americano, which is made in reverse order to the long black – coffee first, water second.

This coffee originated during World War 2 when American girls would pour hot water into espresso to try and make it like the coffee they were used to back home.

90mL cup, 1 shot (30mL) espresso, 1-2 teaspoons of hot or cold milk

'Macchiato' means marked or stained. Espresso macchiato is a single espresso 'stained' with a small amount (1–2 teaspoons) of hot or cold milk, usually with a small amount of foamed milk on top. The foamed milk was traditionally added to show the beverage had a little milk in it, so it wasn't confused with an espresso on serving. This coffee can also be served as a long macchiato, that is, a double espresso stained with a small amount of hot or cold milk.

MACCHIATO

1 Firmly tamp 1 tablespoon of ground coffee to ensure that the water flow is restricted.

2 The pour/extraction should take about 15–20 seconds.

3 Serve in a 90mL glass or ceramic cup with a layer of golden crema on top. Add a dash of cold milk before serving.

NOTE To make long macchiato, use 2 tablespoons of ground coffee and use a twin group head for an even extraction.

LATTE MACCHIATO

Latte macchiato literally means 'stained milk', where steamed white milk gets 'stained' by the addition of espresso. Latte macchiato differs from a caffè latte in that the espresso is added to the milk, rather than the other way around; it features more foam, rather than just hot milk; only a half-shot or less of espresso is used; and the drink is usually layered, not mixed all together.

Piccolo latte is a variant of caffe latte. It is a single espresso shot in a machiatto glass, which is then filled with steamed milk in the same fashion as a caffè latte. This results in a 60mL drink, with a 1:1 ratio of coffee to steamed milk, and about 5mm of foam on the top.

PICCOLO LATTE

1 Firmly tamp 1 tablespoon of ground coffee.

2 The pour should be ½ of the glass.

3 Add 30mL fresh milk that is hot enough to drink almost immediately rather than waiting for it to cool.

4 Scoop milk froth to the top of the glass.

5 Serve in a 90mL cup or glass.

NOTE Create coffee art on top if you wish (see pages 28–57).

Caffè Latte

160mL cup, ⅓ espresso (1 shot), ⅔ steamed milk, 12mm milk froth

In Italy, the caffè latte is traditionally a breakfast drink, prepared at home. Outside Italy it is a standard (30mL) or double (60mL) shot espresso, filled with steamed milk and a layer of foamed milk (approx 12mm) on top.

Caffè latte is an Italian term for a double serving of espresso with steamed milk. Café au lait in French, café con leche in Spanish and kaffee mit milch in German are the same thing.

The caffè latte serving is roughly one-third espresso to two-thirds steamed milk, served in a 160mL ceramic glass or a wide-mouthed glass. Lattes are also served embellished with flavourings added before espresso, or steamed with milk.

In Italy if you ordered a 'latte' you would receive a glass of milk.

Caffè latte is similar to a cappuccino, the difference is that a cappuccino consists of espresso and steamed milk with a 2cm layer of thick milk foam (see page 90).

Another similar drink, which originated in Australia and New Zealand is the flat white, which is served in a smaller ceramic cup, with creamy steamed milk poured over a single shot of espresso, holding back the lighter froth on the top of the milk (see page 88).

CAFFÈ LATTE

1 Firmly tamp 1 tablespoon of ground coffee.

2 The pour should be ⅓ of the glass.

3 Add ⅔ fresh milk that is hot enough to drink almost immediately rather than waiting for it to cool.

4 Scoop milk froth to the top of the glass.

5 Serve in a 160mL cup or glass.

NOTE Create coffee art on top if you wish (see pages 28–57).

Flat White

160mL cup, ⅓ espresso (1 shot), ⅔ steamed milk

The flat white originated in Australia and New Zealand during the early 1980s. It is prepared by pouring steamed milk from the bottom of a steaming jug over a single shot of espresso.

The drink is typically served in 160mL ceramic cups. To achieve the flat, no-froth texture the steamed milk is poured from the bottom of the jug, holding back the lighter froth on top in order to access the milk with smaller bubbles, making the drink smooth and velvety in texture and keeping the crema intact.

FLAT WHITE

1 Firmly tamp 1 tablespoon of ground coffee.

2 The pour/extraction should take about 15–20 seconds and should be about ⅓ of the cup.

3 Add ⅔ fresh hot milk.

4 Serve in a 160mL cup or glass.

NOTE Create coffee art on top if you wish (see pages 28–57).

Cappuccino

160mL cup, ⅓ espresso (1 shot), ⅓ steamed milk, ⅓ milk froth

The origin of the word 'cappuccino' dates back over 500 years to the Capuchin order of friars. The order's name derives from its long, pointed cowl or 'cappuccino', a derivative of 'cappuccio' meaning 'hood' in Italian. It has long been debated as to the link between the Capuchin monks and the cappuccino drink, but it is said that the coffee was named after the friars because the colour of the coffee resembled the colour of their habit. The first use of the word cappuccino in English was recorded in 1948.

Made with one-third espresso, one-third milk and one-third creamy, heavy, dense foam (not light, bubbly, tasteless froth). Usually served in a 145mL ceramic cappuccino cup.

Steamed milk at the bottom of the frothing jug is poured over the espresso, and the froth on top of the jug is spooned on top to cap the cappuccino and retain the heat. Cappuccino is often garnished with a light sprinkle of chocolate or cocoa, cinnamon, nutmeg, vanilla powder or coloured sugar crystals.

CAPPUCCINO

1 Firmly tamp 1 tablespoon of ground coffee.

2 The pour/extraction should take about 15–20 seconds and should be about ⅓ of the cup.

3 Add ⅓ fresh hot milk.

4 Add ⅓ milk froth, which can sit higher than the rim of the cup.

5 Garnish with a sprinkle of chocolate powder.

6 Serve in a cup or glass.

NOTE Create coffee art on top if you wish (see pages 28–76).

Mocha

250mL cup, ⅓ espresso, ⅔ steamed milk, 1 teaspoon chocolate powder

Caffè mocha takes its name from the Red Sea coastal town of Mocha, Yemen, which as far back as the fifteenth century was a dominant exporter of coffee, especially to areas around the Arabian Peninsula.

A caffè mocha is a variant of a caffè latte. Like a latte, it is typically one-third espresso and two-thirds steamed milk, but a portion of chocolate is added, typically in the form of sweet cocoa powder, although many varieties use chocolate syrup. Mochas can contain dark or milk chocolate.

Like cappuccino, mochas contain the well-known milk froth on top, although they are sometimes served with whipped cream instead.

They are usually topped with a dusting of either cinnamon or cocoa powder. Marshmallows may also be added on top for flavour and decoration.

A variant is white caffè mocha, made with white chocolate instead of milk or dark. There are also variants of the drink that mix the two syrups – this mixture is referred to by several names, including black and white mocha, tan mocha, tuxedo mocha and zebra.

MOCHA

1 Pour one teaspoon of drinking chocolate power in a 250mL coffee cup.

2 Firmly tamp 1 tablespoon of ground coffee.

3 Fill the coffee to about ⅓ of the cup. Stir.

4 Top with steamed milk.

5 Sprinkle with chocolate powder.

NOTE Create coffee art on top if you wish (see pages 28–76).

Vienna Coffee

90mL cup, 2 shots espresso, whipped cream

Legend has it that soldiers of the Polish-Habsburg army, while liberating Vienna from the second Turkish siege in 1683, come across a number of sacks of strange beans, which they first thought were camel feed and wanted to destroy. The Polish king granted the sacks to a Polish noble named Franz Georg Kolschitzky, who was instrumental in defeating the Turkish. He opened a coffee house called the Blue Bottle, and began serving coffee as it was prepared in Constantinople (a concoction of pulp and water). The Viennese did not take to this and, after experimentation, Kolschitzky decided to filter the coffee and add cream and honey. Success was immediate.

Vienna coffee is a popular cream-based coffee. It is made by preparing strong shots of espresso into a standard cup or glass and topping with cream (instead of milk or sugar). The coffee is drunk through the cream top.

VIENNA COFFEE

1 Firmly tamp 2 tablespoons of ground coffee to ensure that the water flow is restricted.

2 The pour/extraction should take about 15–20 seconds.

3 Serve in a 90mL glass with whipped cream on top and dusted with cocoa powder.

Iced Coffee

400mL glass, 1 scoop ice cream, ⅓ espresso, ⅔ cold milk, whipped fresh cream

Iced coffee can be a refreshing afternoon treat. If it's really hot outside and you want to cool down but still get your caffeine and coffee flavour, iced coffee is the way to go.

There are many variations of iced coffee, depending on which country you are in. In Australia, it is usually chilled coffee and milk with ice cream and/or whipped cream.

In Canada, it is known as an iced cappuccino or ice capps and it is a frozen coffee-flavoured slushie mixed with cream.

In Greece, there is a variation called a frappé. It is whipped in an electric mixer to create the foam on top. Milk is optional.

Many Italian cafes serve caffè freddo, which is straight espresso kept in the freezer and served as a slushie.

Thai iced coffee is strong black coffee sweetened with sugar, heavy cream and cardamom, quickly cooled and served over ice.

Vietnamese iced coffee is drip coffee with condensed milk over ice.

Most countries also have commercial iced coffees available as well. These are usually sweetened coffee-flavoured milk drinks.

ICED COFFEE

1 Firmly tamp 2 tablespoons of ground coffee to ensure that the water flow is restricted.

2 The pour/extraction should take about 15–20 seconds.

3 Transfer the hot coffee to a carafe or pitcher.

4 Refrigerate until cold, about 2–3 hours.

5 Add 1 scoop of ice cream in a tall or milkshake glass.

6 Add cold coffee to glass until half-full – for a weaker serve add less coffee.

7 Pour cold milk to 1cm under the brim of the glass and stir a couple of times.

8 Finish with whipped or ice cream and garnish with chocolate powder and coffee beans.

Iced Chocolate

400mL glass, 2 tablespoons drinking chocolate, 250mL cold milk,
whipped cream or ice cream

Iced chocolate is a wonderful way to get your chocolate fix in hot weather – when a hot chocolate just won't do!

ICED CHOCOLATE

1 Mix the desired amount of drinking chocolate with a little hot water or milk to make a smooth, thick liquid.

2 Drizzle the liquid decoratively around the inside of a tall glass.

3 Add some ice.

4 Pour cold milk to 1cm under the brim of the glass.

5 Top with whipped or ice cream and dust with chocolate powder.

A variation of this drink is iced mocha, where chilled coffee is mixed into the chocolate, topped up with milk and served with ice cream and/or whipped cream. There are also many variations of iced teas, with or without milk.

ICED MOCHA

1 Firmly tamp 2 tablespoons of ground coffee to ensure that the water flow is restricted.

2 The pour/extraction should take about 15–20 seconds.

3 Combine the hot coffee and 1½ tablespoons brown sugar in a large measuring cup and stir until the brown sugar dissolves. Stir in chocolate syrup. Transfer to a carafe or pitcher.

4 Refrigerate until cold, about 2–3 hours.

5 Combine the chilled coffee, ½ cup ice-cold milk and ¼ teaspoon vanilla extract. Stir to blend. Pour into the glass, adding a small handful of crushed ice

6 Finish with whipped or ice cream and garnish with grated chocolate.

Hot Chocolate

250mL cup, 1 tablespoon drinking chocolate, 250mL hot milk

Hot chocolate is a heated beverage typically consisting of shaved chocolate, melted chocolate buds or cocoa powder, heated milk or water and sugar.

Drinking chocolate is similar to hot chocolate (or cocoa), but is made from melted chocolate shavings or paste rather than a powdered mix that's soluble in water.

The first chocolate beverage is believed to have been created by the Mayan peoples around 2000 years ago, and a cocoa beverage was an essential part of Aztec culture by 1400 AD. The beverage became popular in Europe after being introduced from Mexico, and has undergone multiple changes since then. Until the 19th century, hot chocolate was even used medicinally to treat ailments such as stomach diseases. Today, hot chocolate is consumed throughout the world and comes in multiple variations including the very thick, dense chocolate served in Italy.

HOT CHOCOLATE

1 Mix 1 tablespoon of drinking chocolate in a mug with a little hot water or milk to make a smooth, thick liquid.

2 Fill the mug with hot frothed milk and sprinkle with chocolate. Serve with marshmallow if desired.

ITALIAN HOT CHOCOLATE

1 Mix 60mL unsweetened cocoa, 3 tablespoons sugar and ½ teaspoon arrowroot together until thoroughly blended.

2 Add 60mL milk to a medium saucepan and set over low heat. Whisk in the cocoa mixture until thoroughly incorporated and no lumps remain. Add the rest of the milk.

3 Cook, stirring constantly, over medium-low heat, until the mixture is thickened, about 10 minutes.

4 Once the cocoa has thickened, stir in a hint of additional flavourings before serving – ⅛ teaspoon vanilla or almond extract or a teaspoon of Grand Marnier would be nice. Dust with cinnamon or nutmeg.

NOTE Alternatively, you can substitute half the liquid with coffee to make a nice mocha.

Babycino

A babycino (also known as a steamer) is a drink of frothed milk but no coffee. It is primarily marketed towards children. It can have flavoured syrups added, or be topped with chocolate sprinkle or marshmallows.

BABYCINO

1 Drizzle flavoured syrup decoratively around the inside of a glass.

2 Fill glass with hot or warm frothed milk.

3 Add marshmallow if desired.

4 Sprinkle with chocolate powder.

FLAVOURED SYRUPS The early 1990s saw the growth of speciality coffee and with this came the increased usage of flavoured syrups to flavour lattes and other hot drinks. It was then that DaVinci Gourmet developed its range. The goal was to develop syrup that would retain taste and consistency in hot drinks such as lattes and mochas, while also being just as flavourful in cold drinks such as cocktails and Italian sodas. Now flavoured syrups are an essential part of any drink menu, and offer a powerful tool for reaching customers. The flavour category continues to grow and invites non-coffee drinkers or new entrants into the market. Flavours are fun, easy to use and offer endless ways to customize menus and drinks. When using flavoured syrup in a hot drink, make sure you add the syrup first, and extract your coffee into the syrup – this will activate the flavour component in the syrup and make sure it is evenly dispersed throughout the cup.

Chai Latte

WHAT IS CHAI TEA?

Chai, pronounced with a long 'i' as in the word tie, is the actual word for tea in many countries. Chai tea is quickly becoming extremely popular in the West as people are becoming exposed to it in coffee and tea houses.

Chai tea is a rich and complex beverage that has been savoured for centuries in many parts of the world, especially India.

In its most basic form, chai is black tea that is brewed strong with a combination of spices and is diluted with milk and sugar.

The spices vary from recipe to recipe, but usually consist of cinnamon, cardamom, cloves, pepper and ginger. Chai tea is traditionally consumed hot and sweet. The sweetness is needed to bring out the full flavors of the spices.

A chai latte is just the spiced tea mixed with milk that's steamed from an espresso machine. Practise making velvety steamed milk and always use fresh ingredients – this will ensure that you make the perfect chai latte.

CHAI LATTE

1 Place 190mL water, 1 stick of cinnamon, 4 cardamom pods, 4 whole cloves, and 4mm fresh ginger root (thinly sliced) in a pot and bring to the boil.

2 Cover, lower heat and simmer for 10 minutes.

3 Add 3 teaspoons sugar and again bring to simmer.

4 Next, add 1½ teaspoons of tea leaves, remove from heat and cover.

5 Let steep for 3 minutes, then strain.

6 Add 80mL fresh milk that is hot enough to drink almost immediately rather than waiting for it to cool.

7 Scoop the milk froth to the top of the glass.

makes 1

Affogato Agave

PREPARATION 5 mins

2 scoops vanilla bean ice cream

60mL espresso coffee

2 tablespoons Patron XO Café Tequila, Frangelico or Kahlúa

1 teaspoon hazelnuts, chopped

1 Put the ice cream in the glass and drown it with the espresso coffee.

2 Pour over your choice of liqueur.

3 Garnish with chopped hazelnuts.

NOTE Developed by the 2010 Australian Barista Champion of Coffee Cocktails, Mitch Faulkner.

makes 1

Café Agave

PREPARATION 5 mins

2 tablespoons Patron XO Café Tequila

2 tablespoons cocoa liqueur

60mL espresso coffee

60mL cream

1 chocolate flake

1 Shake all the ingredients, except chocolate flake, with ice and strain into the glass.

2 Serve in a martini glass, garnished with chocolate flakes.

NOTE Developed by the 2010 Australian Barista Champion of Coffee Cocktails, Mitch Faulkner.

makes 1

Caribbean Coffee

PREPARATION 5 mins

2 tablespoons dark rum

150mL hot black coffee

3 tablespoons whipped cream

1 Pour the rum and coffee into an Irish coffee cup and sweeten to taste.

2 Float the cream on top and sprinkle with grated chocolate.

2 Garnish with chocolate-coated coffee beans and serve.

VARIATIONS

Alternatively, you can make this by substituting Kahlúa for the dark rum.

makes 1

Blackjack

PREPARATION 5 mins

MIXERS

2 tablespoons Kirsch

60mL fresh coffee

2 teaspoons brandy

1 Stir all the ingredients with crushed ice in a mixing glass, strain, then pour into a cocktail glass.

2 Serve garnished with coffee granules.

VARIATIONS

Alternatively, you can make *Roulette* by substituting vodka for the Kirsch.

makes 1

Café Oscar

PREPARATION 5 mins

| 1 tablespoon Kahlúa |
| 1 tablespoon Amaretto di Galliano |
| hot coffee |
| double cream |
| 1 scoop vanilla ice cream |

1 Pour the spirits into a glass, then top up with coffee.

2 Float the cream on top. Garnish with the ice cream.

VARIATIONS

Alternatively, you can make *Café Maria* by substituting Tia Maria and Galliano for the Kahlúa and Amaretto.

Irish Coffee

PREPARATION 5 mins

MIXERS

1 teaspoon brown sugar

2 tablespoons Baileys

hot black coffee

2 tablespoons fresh whipped
cream

chocolate flakes or chocolate
powder

1 Stir the sugar into the Baileys. Top up
with coffee. Float the fresh cream on top,
then garnish with chocolate.

VARIATIONS

Alternatively, you can make Irish coffee with whisky by substituting a good
Irish whisky such as Tullamore Dew or Jameson's for the Baileys. Other liqueur
coffees are: French – brandy, English – gin, Russian – vodka, American – Bourbon,
Calypso – dark rum, Jamaican – Tia Maria, Parisienne – Grand Marnier, Mexican
– Kahlúa, Monks – Benedictine, Scottish – Scotch, Canadian – rye.

makes 1

Coffee Break

PREPARATION 5 mins

125mL hot black coffee

1 tablespoon brandy

1 tablespoon Kahlúa

3 tablespoons whipped cream

1 maraschino cherry

1 Pour the coffee and liquors into an Irish coffee cup and sweeten to taste.

2 Float the cream on top, add a maraschino cherry and serve.

VARIATIONS

Alternatively, you can make *Peppermint Break* by substituting crème de menthe for brandy.

Coffee Nudge

PREPARATION 5 mins

2 teaspoons dark crème
 de cacao

2 teaspoons Kahlúa

1 tablespoon brandy

250mL hot coffee

60mL whipped cream

1 Combine the liquors with the coffee and top with whipped cream.

VARIATIONS

Alternatively, you can make *Liquorice Coffee* by substituting black sambuca for the brandy and coffee liqueur.

Iced Cappuccino

PREPARATION 5 mins

90mL strong espresso

60mL milk

2 tablespoons vanilla syrup

1 tablespoon Kahlúa

1 tablespoon caramel syrup

60mL cream

1 Blend all the ingredients with 2 scoops of ice. Pour into a poco grande glass.

Mocha Mudslide Milkshake

PREPARATION 5 mins

250mL milk

150g sliced ripe banana

2 tablespoons sugar

30mL espresso

50mL vanilla yoghurt

1 Place the milk, banana, sugar and espresso in a blender and blend until smooth. Freeze in a blender container for 1 hour or until slightly frozen. Loosen the frozen mixture from the sides of the blender container, add the yoghurt and blend until smooth. Garnish with extra banana slices. Serve immediately.

makes 1

Galliano Hotshot

PREPARATION 5 mins

2 tablespoons Galliano

2 tablespoons hot coffee

1 tablespoon double cream

1 Pour the Galliano into a shot glass, then carefully pour the coffee on top. Finally, gently spoon the cream on top of the coffee layer.

makes 1

Royale Coffee

PREPARATION 5 mins

2 tablespoons Cognac

150mL hot black coffee

3 tablespoons whipped cream

1 teaspoon grated chocolate

1 Add the coffee and Cognac to an Irish coffee cup and sweeten to taste. Gently float the whipped cream on top, sprinkle with grated chocolate and serve.

Royale Coffee, page 125

Coffee Choc Bit Biscuits, page 129

makes 18

Coffee Choc Bit Biscuits

PREPARATION 15 mins   COOKING 15 mins

125g butter

100g caster sugar

70g brown sugar, firmly packed

1 tablespoon instant coffee

1 egg

200g self-raising flour

1 cup choc bits

1 Preheat oven to 180°C.

2 Cream the butter and sugars. Beat in the coffee, then the egg.

3 Stir in the flour and choc chip bits until mixed.

4 Drop spoonfuls of the mixture onto a greased baking tray and bake for 10–15 minutes. Allow to cool on tray.

makes 12

Mocha Meringues

PREPARATION 1 hr 15 mins   COOKING 40 mins

1 egg white

1/8 teaspoon cream of tartar

2 tablespoons white sugar

1/4 teaspoon vanilla extract

1 tablespoon cocoa

1/2 teaspoon instant coffee powder

1 Preheat oven to 120°C.

2 Beat the egg white and cream of tartar at high speed until soft peaks form. Gradually add the sugar, vanilla, cocoa and coffee.

3 Drop the mixture onto a foil-lined baking sheet in 12 mounds, about 5cm apart.

4 Bake for 40 minutes or until firm. Turn off oven and let the meringues cool in oven for 1 hour. Do not open oven door while the meringues are cooling.

makes 25

Coffee Kisses

PREPARATION 12 mins   COOKING 12 mins

250g butter, at room
  temperature

70g icing sugar, sifted

2 teaspoons instant coffee
  powder, dissolved in

1 tablespoon hot water,
  then cooled

225g flour, sifted

3 tablespoons bittersweet
  chocolate, melted

1 Preheat oven to 180°C.

2 Place the butter and icing sugar in a bowl and beat until light and fluffy. Stir in the coffee mixture and flour.

3 Spoon the mixture into a piping bag fitted with a medium star nozzle and pipe 2cm rounds of mixture 2cm apart on greased baking trays. Bake for 10–12 minutes or until lightly browned. Stand on trays for 5 minutes before removing to wire racks to cool completely.

4 Join the biscuits with a little melted chocolate, then dust with icing sugar.

NOTE These coffee-flavoured biscuits have a similar texture to shortbread, making the dough perfect for piping. For something different, pipe 5cm lengths instead of rounds. Rather than sandwiching the biscuits together with chocolate, you may prefer to leave them plain and simply dust with icing sugar.

makes 13 pairs

Chocolate Melting Moments

PREPARATION 10 mins   **COOKING** 20 mins

250g butter, at room
 temperature

70g icing sugar

2 teaspoons vanilla extract

175g plain flour

3 tablespoons cocoa powder

40g cornflour

CHOCOLATE CREAM

50g butter, at room
 temperature

1 tablespoon cocoa powder

½ teaspoon vanilla extract

1 teaspoon instant coffee
 powder

100g icing sugar

1 Preheat oven to 180°C.

2 Beat the butter and icing sugar together until fluffy.

3 Add the vanilla. Sift in the flour, cocoa and cornflour. Beat with a wooden spoon to combine.

4 Measure tablespoonfuls of mixture onto a greased oven tray. Flatten with a fork.

5 Bake for 15–20 minutes or until just starting to colour.

6 Cool on a wire rack. Sandwich together with chocolate cream.

CHOCOLATE CREAM
1 Place the butter in a bowl. Beat in the cocoa, vanilla, coffee and icing sugar until smooth.

makes 30

Coffee Pecan Biscuits

PREPARATION 40 mins   COOKING 18 mins

125g butter, at room
  temperature

100g caster sugar

½ teaspoon vanilla extract

1 egg, at room temperature

2 teaspoons instant coffee
  powder

225g plain flour

1 teaspoon baking powder

1 tablespoon milk

250g pecans, finely chopped

COFFEE ICING

100g icing sugar

1 tablespoon boiling water

1 tablespoon butter, at room
  temperature

2 teaspoons instant coffee
  powder

1 Using an electric mixer, beat the butter, sugar and vanilla in a small bowl until pale and creamy. Add the egg and coffee and mix until well combined. Sift the flour and baking powder over the butter mixture. Add the milk and stir until just combined. Divide the dough in half.

2 Roll each piece of dough into a 45mm diameter log. Roll the logs in the chopped pecans until well coated. Wrap each log in cling film. Refrigerate for at least 30 minutes or until firm.

3 Preheat oven to 180°C. Line 2 baking trays with baking paper.

4 Using a sharp knife, carefully cut the logs into 15mm slices. Place on the lined baking trays. Bake for 15–18 minutes or until a light golden colour. Allow to cool for about 5 minutes, then transfer to wire racks to cool completely.

5 Make the coffee icing. Sift the icing sugar into a bowl. Combine the boiling water, butter and coffee in a separate bowl and stir until the coffee is dissolved. Add to the icing sugar and stir until mixture is smooth.

6 Drop 1 teaspoon of icing onto the centre of each biscuit. Top with a pecan. Allow the icing to set before serving.

makes 14–16

Bourbon Biscuits

PREPARATION 30 mins   COOKING 20 mins

60g butter

50g caster sugar

1 tablespoon golden syrup

115g plain flour

15g cocoa powder

½ teaspoon baking soda

FILLING

50g butter

90g icing sugar, sifted

1 tablespoon cocoa powder

1 teaspoon instant coffee
 powder

1 Preheat the oven to 160°C. Cream the butter and sugar together very thoroughly, then beat in the syrup.

2 Sift the flour, cocoa and baking soda together, then work into the creamed mixture to make a stiff paste.

3 Knead well, and roll out on a lightly floured surface into an oblong strip about 5mm thick. If the rolled dough is too long for your baking tray, cut it in half. Place on a lightly buttered baking tray covered with greaseproof paper. Bake for 15–20 minutes.

4 Cut into fingers of equal width while still warm. Cool on a wire rack while you prepare the filling.

FILLING

1 Beat the butter until soft, then add the sugar, cocoa and coffee. Beat until smooth. Sandwich the cooled fingers with a layer of filling.

makes 24

Brazilian Coffee Biscuits

PREPARATION 20 mins   COOKING 10 mins

100g butter
100g soft dark brown sugar
100g caster sugar
1 egg
1½ teaspoons vanilla extract
1 tablespoon milk
330g plain flour
½ teaspoon salt
¼ teaspoon baking soda
¼ teaspoon baking powder
2 tablespoons instant coffee powder

1 Preheat oven to 200°C. Line 2 baking trays with greaseproof paper.

2 Beat the butter, brown sugar, caster sugar, egg, vanilla and milk until fluffy.

3 In a separate bowl, mix the flour, salt, baking soda, baking powder and instant coffee. Add to the sugar mixture and mix thoroughly.

4 Shape the dough in 2cm balls. If too soft to shape, chill for a while. Place the balls 5cm apart on the baking trays.

5 Flatten to 1cm thickness with a fork or glass dipped in sugar. Bake for 8–10 minutes until lightly browned.

makes 48

Macadamia Coconut Squares

PREPARATION 30 mins   COOKING 1 hr 10 mins

250g butter

300g brown sugar, firmly packed

1 tablespoon instant coffee powder

½ teaspoon ground cinnamon

½ teaspoon salt

2 cups plain flour

3 eggs

2 teaspoons vanilla extract

2 cups desiccated coconut

2 cups chopped toasted macadamias

1 Preheat oven to 170°C.

2 Lightly butter a 22 x 33cm baking pan and set aside.

3 In a large mixing bowl, beat the butter, 150g brown sugar, the instant coffee powder, ¼ teaspoon cinnamon and ¼ teaspoon salt until light and fluffy. Stir in the flour half a cup at a time, blending well after each addition.

4 Spread evenly in the prepared pan. Bake for 20 minutes. Cool in the pan on a wire rack for 15 minutes.

5 In a large bowl, beat the eggs and vanilla with remaining 150g brown sugar, ¼ teaspoon cinnamon and ¼ teaspoon salt. Stir in the coconut and macadamias. Spread evenly over cooled baked layer.

6 Bake for 40–50 minutes, or until golden brown and firm to the touch. Use a knife to loosen around the edges while warm.

7 Cool completely in the pan on a wire rack. Cut into 48 squares, cutting 6 strips one way and 8 strips the other way.

8 Store in an airtight container at room temperature.

makes about 75

Cappuccino Crisps

PREPARATION 1 hr   **COOKING** 10 mins

250g unsalted butter

200g white sugar

6 tablespoons cocoa powder

¼ teaspoon ground cinnamon

1 egg

2 teaspoons instant coffee
  powder

1 teaspoon vanilla extract

225g plain flour

ICING

280g icing sugar

60mL hot milk

3 tablespoons butter

1 tablespoon golden syrup

2 teaspoons instant coffee
  powder

1 teaspoon vanilla extract

1 teaspoon olive oil

¼ teaspoon salt

1 Beat the butter, sugar, cocoa and cinnamon in a large bowl, then beat in the egg.

2 Stir the coffee powder, vanilla and 1 teaspoon water in a cup to dissolve the coffee. Beat into the butter mixture.

3 On a low speed, beat in the flour until just blended. Divide the dough in half and shape into a disc. Wrap and chill until firm.

4 Preheat oven to 190°C. Have ready a 75mm star cookie cutter.

5 Roll the dough on a well-floured rolling surface to about 5mm thickness. Cut out stars and place 25mm apart on an ungreased cookie sheet.

6 Bake for 8 minutes or until crisp.

7 To make the icing, put the icing sugar in a medium bowl, gradually stir in the hot milk until smooth, stir in butter until blended, then add the remaining ingredients and 1 tablespoon hot water. Spoon the icing into a corner of a plastic bag, snip off the tip of the corner and drizzle a zigzag design on the cookies.

makes 25

Chocolate Coffee Tuiles

PREPARATION 20 mins   **COOKING** 5 mins

2 egg whites

100g caster sugar

½ teaspoon instant coffee

 powder, dissolved in

 ½ teaspoon water

1 teaspoon vanilla extract

1 tablespoon cocoa powder,

 sifted

1¼ tablespoons milk

60g butter, melted and cooled

1 Preheat oven to 170°C.

2 Place the egg whites in a bowl and beat until soft peaks form. Gradually add the sugar, beating well after each addition, until the mixture is glossy and the sugar dissolved. Fold the coffee mixture, vanilla, cocoa powder, milk and butter into the egg white mixture.

3 Drop spoonfuls of the mixture 10cm apart onto greased baking tray and bake for 5 minutes or until the edges are set. Remove from the tray and wrap each biscuit around the handle of a wooden spoon. Allow to cool for 2 minutes or until set. Repeat with the remaining mixture.

makes 12

Coffee Biscuits

PREPARATION 15 mins   COOKING 30 mins

110g butter

85g sugar

1 egg

1 teaspoon coffee essence

225g self-raising flour

COFFEE ICING

50g butter, softened

90g icing sugar

2 teaspoons instant coffee
 powder

1 Preheat oven to 180°C.

2 Cream the butter and sugar. Add the egg and beat well. Add the coffee essence and flour and combine well.

3 Roll into balls and flatten with a fork.

4 Bake for 30 minutes. When cold, join with coffee icing.

COFFEE ICING

1 Beat the butter, icing sugar and coffee together until smooth.

Mocha Dessert Cake, page 166

makes 12 slices

Cappuccino Cheesecake

PREPARATION 30 mins   COOKING 1 hr 20 mins

BASE

150g finely chopped nuts
(almonds, walnuts)

2 tablespoons sugar

50g butter, melted

FILLING

1kg cream cheese, at room
temperature

200g sugar

3 tablespoons plain flour

4 large eggs

250mL sour cream

1 tablespoon instant coffee
powder

¼ teaspoon ground cinnamon

1 Preheat oven to 160°C.

BASE
2 Combine the nuts, sugar and butter, press onto the bottom of a 23cm springform tin. Bake for 10 minutes, remove from oven and allow to cool. Increase oven temperature to 230°C.

FILLING
1 Combine the cream cheese, sugar and flour in an electric mixer, mix on medium speed until well blended. Add the eggs, one at a time, mixing well after each addition. Blend in the sour cream.

2 Dissolve the coffee and cinnamon in 60mL boiling water. Cool, then gradually add to the cream cheese mixture, mixing until well blended. Pour over the base.

3 Bake for 10 minutes. Reduce oven temperature to 120°C and continue baking for 1 hour.

4 Loosen the cake from the rim, allow to cool before removing. Chill. Serve topped with whipped cream and coffee beans.

makes 12 slices

Cocomo Cheesecake

PREPARATION 30 mins   COOKING 1 hr 15 mins

BASE

120g digestive biscuits, finely crushed

3 tablespoons sugar

50g butter, melted

FILLING

60g cooking chocolate

40g butter

500g cream cheese, at room temperature

250g sugar

5 large eggs

125g flaked coconut

TOPPING

250mL sour cream

2 tablespoons sugar

2 tablespoons passionfruit liqueur

1 teaspoon instant coffee powder

1 Preheat oven to 175°C.

BASE
1 Combine the crumbs, sugar and butter, press onto the bottom of a 23cm springform tin. Bake for 10 minutes.

FILLING
1 Melt the chocolate and butter over a low heat, stirring until smooth.

2 Combine the cream cheese and sugar in an electric mixer, mix on medium speed until well blended. Add the eggs one at a time, mixing well after each addition. Blend in the chocolate mixture and coconut, pour over the base.

3 Bake for 60 minutes or until set.

TOPPING
1 Combine the sour cream, sugar, liqueur and coffee, spread over the cheesecake.

2 Reduce heat to 150°C and bake for 5 minutes.

3 Loosen the cake from the rim of the tin, cool before removing. Chill and serve dusted with cocoa powder.

makes 12

Coffee and Walnut Surprises

PREPARATION 20 mins   **COOKING** 20 mins

250g butter, at room
 temperature

100g sugar

2 eggs

2 tablespoons Baileys Irish
 Cream

100g chopped walnuts

2 tablespoons instant coffee
 powder

175g self-raising flour

SAUCE

100g caster sugar

250mL thickened cream

1 tablespoon instant coffee
 powder

1 Preheat oven to 180°C.

2 Beat the butter and sugar until light and fluffy, stir in the eggs, Baileys and walnuts. Sift in the coffee and flour and mix to combine.

3 Divide the mixture evenly into a lightly buttered 12-hole muffin or friand tin.

4 Bake for 15–20 minutes or until risen and firm.

5 Leave to cool for 10 minutes, then remove from the tin.

SAUCE

1 Heat sugar and 60mL water in saucepan until the mixture is boiling and the sugar dissolves. Reduce the heat, simmer until golden. Add the cream and coffee. Bring to the boil and simmer until the toffee dissolves and the sauce thickens. Pour over the surprises. Serve with tea or coffee and Irish cream liqueur.

serves 8–10

Espresso Cake

PREPARATION 30 mins   COOKING 1 hr

70g finely ground espresso
coffee beans

200g butter

250g sugar

3 eggs

1 tablespoon vanilla extract

225g plain flour

3 teaspoons baking powder

COFFEE CREAM

300mL thickened cream

1 tablespoon icing sugar

2 tablespoons very strong
espresso coffee

1 Preheat oven to 180°C.

2 Pour 1 cup boiling water over half the ground coffee beans and leave to steep for 5 minutes. Strain the liquid from the beans and pour over the butter in a large bowl, stirring until the butter melts. Discard the strained beans.

3 Mix in the sugar, eggs and vanilla and beat with a wooden spoon until combined. Sift the flour and baking powder into the mixture and mix in with the remaining ground coffee beans.

4 Pour the mixture into a baking-paper-lined 20cm square cake tin. Bake for 50–55 minutes or until the cake springs back when lightly touched.

5 Cool in the tin for 10 minutes before turning onto a cooling rack. Dust with cinnamon.

6 To make the coffee cream, whip cream until soft, then beat in icing sugar and coffee. Serve with the cake.

serves 12–16

Modern Anzac Cake

PREPARATION 30 mins   COOKING 1 hr 20 mins

125g butter, at room temperature

200g sugar

2 eggs

1 teaspoon vanilla extract

85g ground almonds

3 tablespoons cocoa powder

30g shredded coconut

200g self-raising flour

320g sour cream

125mL espresso coffee

TOPPING

200g sugar

4 tablespoons golden syrup

80g butter

150g flaked almonds

30g shredded coconut

30g rolled oats

1 Preheat the oven to 160°C and butter and line a 24cm cake tin.

2 Cream the butter and sugar together until thick and pale, then add the eggs one at a time, beating well after each addition. Add the vanilla and mix well to combine.

3 In a separate bowl, mix together the almonds, cocoa, coconut and flour.

4 Fold half the flour mixture into the batter with the sour cream and combine gently. Add the remaining flour mixture with the coffee and mix well.

5 Bake in the preheated oven for 1 hour until puffed and cooked through.

6 Meanwhile, prepare the topping. Place 150mL water and the sugar in a small saucepan and heat gently while stirring to dissolve the sugar granules. When the mixture begins to boil, stop stirring and simmer for about 5 minutes, brushing down the sides of the pan with a pastry brush. When the mixture is pale gold, remove from the heat and stir in the golden syrup, butter, almonds, coconut and rolled oats and stir thoroughly, returning to the heat if necessary to help you mix the ingredients well. After the cake has cooked for 1 hour, remove from the oven and pour this mixture over the cake, then return to the oven for 10 minutes or until the topping has set.

7 Remove the cake from the oven and allow to cool in the tin for 10 minutes. Use a knife to loosen any toffee from the sides of the tin, then remove the cake and cool completely on a wire rack.

Sticky Date Cupcakes

PREPARATION 12 mins   COOKING 20 mins

2 eggs

135g butter, at room
 temperature

175g caster sugar

115g self-raising flour, sifted

400g dates, chopped

2 teaspoons instant coffee
 powder

1 teaspoon baking soda

1 teaspoon vanilla extract

140g ground almond flour

55g walnuts, finely chopped

TOPPING

150g light-brown sugar,
 firmly packed

60g unsalted butter

1 teaspoon vanilla extract

125mL thickened cream

12 dates

1 Preheat the oven to 160°C. Line a 12-cupcake pan with cupcake papers. In a medium bowl, lightly beat the eggs, add the butter and sugar, then mix until light and fluffy.

2 Add 190mL water and the flour, and stir to combine. Add the remaining ingredients. Mix with a wooden spoon for 2 minutes, until light and creamy.

3 Divide the mixture evenly between the cake papers. Bake for 18–20 minutes until risen and firm to the touch. Allow to cool for a few minutes and then transfer to a wire rack. Allow to cool fully before icing.

TOPPING

1 Meanwhile, combine the sugar, butter, vanilla and 1 tablespoon water in a saucepan. Bring to a simmer over medium-low heat, stirring constantly. Without stirring again, simmer for 1 minute. Remove from the heat and allow to cool. Beat the cream until soft peaks form and fold the mixture in. Spoon onto the cupcakes and top with dates.

Torta Tiramisu

PREPARATION 1 hr   COOKING 45 mins

6 egg whites

pinch of salt

230g caster sugar

100g roasted almonds, ground

1 tablespoon icing sugar

40g cornflour

FILLING

7 level teaspoons gelatine

125mL coffee liqueur

125g caster sugar

40g instant coffee powder

500g mascarpone cheese

4 egg yolks

250mL thickened cream,
  whipped

80g dark chocolate,
  finely grated

cocoa powder, for dusting

1 Preheat the oven to 180°C. Lightly butter and line two 24cm springform tins.

2 Firstly, make the meringue bases. Beat the egg whites and salt until stiff peaks form and then gradually add the caster sugar, a little at a time. Beat at top speed for 10 minutes until the sugar is completely dissolved and the mixture is thick and glossy.

3 In a separate bowl, mix the almonds, icing sugar and cornflour, then gently fold into the egg white mixture. Divide the mixture evenly between the cake tins and bake at 180°C for 45 minutes, then cool completely. (If you do not have two 24cm cake tins, bake half the mixture and, when cool, remove from the tin. Re-butter and line the cake tin to bake the remaining mixture.)

4 Place the gelatine and 60mL water in a small bowl and stand in a pan of boiling water to dissolve, or heat in a microwave oven on high for 10 seconds. Place the coffee liqueur, sugar and instant coffee in a saucepan and bring to the boil. Stir in the dissolved gelatine and mix well. Set aside. Place the mascarpone in a mixing bowl and beat in the egg yolks and coffee mixture. Gently fold in the whipped cream and mix gently.

5 To assemble the cake, place one of the meringue bases in the bottom of a 23cm springform pan and pour over half the filling. Smooth, then sprinkle with half the grated chocolate. Top with the second base and press down lightly. Cover with the remaining filling and remaining chocolate. Chill for at least 2 hours. Carefully remove from the sides of the cake tin, then slide the cake off the base. Dust the top of the cake with cocoa powder.

serves 8

Mocha Mousse Roll

PREPARATION 40 mins   COOKING 30 mins

180g dark chocolate, grated

60g butter

5 eggs, separated

3 tablespoons Tia Maria liqueur

60g caster sugar

2 tablespoons cocoa powder, sifted

1 tablespoon instant coffee powder

250mL thickened cream

1 Preheat oven to 180°C. Lightly butter and line with baking paper a Swiss roll tin.

2 Melt the chocolate and butter in a bowl over a bowl of simmering water and stir until smooth.

3 Beat in the egg yolks one at a time, beating well after each addition. Stir in 2 tablespoons Tia Maria.

4 Beat the egg whites in a small bowl until soft peaks form. Gradually add the sugar, beating until the mixture becomes thick and glossy. Fold in the chocolate mixture, stir until well combined.

5 Spread the mixture evenly into the Swiss roll tin. Bake for 30 minutes until firm. Turn out onto a sheet of greaseproof paper, sprinkle with the sifted cocoa. Remove the paper lining and allow to cool.

6 Combine the coffee and 1 tablespoon boiling water, then cool. Beat the cream until soft peaks form, stir in the coffee mixture and remaining Tia Maria. Spread evenly over the cake and roll up lengthways, using paper to help. Refrigerate until firm, then serve sliced.

serves 6–8

Coffee
Sandwich Cake

PREPARATION 1 hr   **COOKING** 35 mins

250g butter, at room
temperature

190g caster sugar

6 eggs, lightly beaten

225g self-raising flour, sifted

ICING

60g butter, softened

100g icing sugar, sifted

½ teaspoon ground cinnamon

2 teaspoons instant coffee
powder, dissolved in
2 teaspoons hot water,
then cooled

FILLING

1 tablespoon coffee-flavoured
liqueur

125mL double cream

1 Preheat oven to 160°C.

2 Place the butter and sugar in a food processor and process until creamy. Add the eggs and flour and process until all the ingredients are combined.

3 Spoon the batter into two buttered and lined 18cm sandwich tins and bake for 30–35 minutes or until golden and cooked when tested with a skewer. Turn the cakes onto wire racks to cool.

ICING

1 Place the butter, icing sugar, cinnamon and coffee mixture in a food processor and process until light and fluffy.

FILLING

1 Beat the cream until soft peaks form and fold the liqueur in.

2 Spread the filling over one cake and top with the remaining cake. Spread the icing over the top of the cake.

serves 6–8

Mocha Dessert Cake

PREPARATION 20 mins   COOKING 1 hr

100g cooking chocolate

150g butter

200g sugar

250mL strong black coffee

115g plain flour

40g cornflour

1 egg

1 Preheat oven to 160°C and line the bottom of a 20cm round cake tin with baking paper.

2 Mix the chocolate, butter, sugar and coffee in a saucepan large enough to mix all the ingredients and heat gently until the butter and chocolate have melted and the mixture is smooth.

3 Remove from the heat. Sift in the flour and cornflour and add the egg. Beat with a wooden spoon until smooth, then pour the mixture into the cake tin.

4 Bake for 50–60 minutes or until the cake is firm. Stand in the tin for 10 minutes before turning onto a wire rack.

5 Serve dusted with cocoa powder and accompanied with fruit.

Mocha Cream, page 169

serves 4

Mocha Cream

PREPARATION 15 mins

375mL thickened cream

1 tablespoon vanilla extract

2 teaspoons instant coffee

  powder, dissolved in

  2 tablespoons water

4 egg whites

100g caster sugar

100g dark chocolate, melted

3 tablespoons Kahlúa

1 Beat the cream with the vanilla essence and coffee until soft peaks form.

2 Whip the egg whites until stiff, then gradually add the sugar and continue to beat until thick and glossy, about 5 minutes.

3 Combine the melted chocolate and Kahlúa with the cream mixture. Gently fold the egg whites into the chocolate and coffee cream mixture until just combined. Spoon into 4 serving glasses and top with coffee beans to garnish.

serves 4

Coffee Chocolate Mousse

PREPARATION 25 mins   COOKING 5 mins

100g dark chocolate, melted

60mL espresso

6 eggs, separated

100g caster sugar

1 Melt the chocolate with the espresso. Beat the egg yolks and sugar until thick and pale. Add the chocolate mixture to the yolks. Beat the egg whites until soft peaks form. Fold the whites through yolk mixture.

2 Put the mousse in the refrigerator for 1 hour before serving. Serve with a dollop of double cream and coffee granules.

serves 4–6

Cappuccino Pie

PREPARATION 30 mins   COOKING 15 mins

BASE

200g packet chocolate
  wheaten biscuits
50g butter, melted
1 tablespoon instant coffee
  powder

FILLING

250mL milk
2 tablespoons instant coffee
  powder
55g sugar
40g cornflour
2 egg yolks

TOPPING

2 egg whites
100g sugar
½ teaspoon cocoa powder
chocolate sticks

1 Preheat oven to 190°C.

2 Crush the biscuits until medium-fine crumbs in a food processor or thick plastic bag. Pour in the melted butter, add the coffee powder and mix to combine. Press the mixture into the base of a 20cm springform pan or loose-bottom cake tin. Refrigerate while preparing the filling.

FILLING

1 Whisk the milk, coffee, sugar and cornflour together. Heat, stirring constantly, until the mixture boils and thickens. Remove from the heat and mix in the egg yolks. Pour into the prepared base.

TOPPING

1 Beat the egg whites until stiff. Gradually beat in the sugar until the mixture is thick and glossy, then spread over the filling.

2 Bake for 10 minutes or until just starting to colour. Dust with the cocoa and garnish with chocolate sticks to serve.

Coffee Pecan Pie

PREPARATION 9 hrs   **COOKING** 50 mins

75g butter

140g white sugar

250mL golden syrup

3 eggs

1 cup pecans, coarsely
chopped

1 teaspoon instant coffee
powder, dissolved in
1 teaspoon water

pinch of salt

1 cup semisweet chocolate
chips

125mL double cream

1 tablespoon icing sugar

¼ teaspoon vanilla extract

PIE CRUST

175g plain flour

125g butter, chopped

60g caster sugar

1 egg yolk

PIE CRUST

1 Combine the flour, butter and sugar in a food processor, pulse until mixture resembles breadcrumbs.

2 Add the egg yolk and enough chilled water to form a dough. Knead lightly, wrap in cling film and refrigerate for 30 minutes.

3 Roll the dough out between 2 sheets of baking paper and line a 22cm, lightly buttered pie dish with the pastry. Keep the crust in the refrigerator until ready to use.

FILLING

1 Preheat oven to 190°C. In a medium saucepan, melt the butter over a low heat. Stir in the sugar and golden syrup and set aside to cool.

2 In a mixing bowl, beat the eggs well. Stir in the chopped pecans and melted butter mixture. Stir in the coffee. Spread the chocolate chips evenly over the bottom of the pie crust.

3 Pour the pecan mixture over the crust. Bake for 45–50 minutes, or until set.

4 Cover and let stand at room temperature for about 8 hours before serving. The pie should be soft.

5 Combine the cream, icing sugar and vanilla in a small mixing bowl. Whip until stiff, then serve with the pie.

makes approximately 750mL

Mocha Ice Cream

PREPARATION 20 mins

4 egg yolks

100g caster sugar

2 tablespoons coffee liqueur

1 tablespoon instant coffee
powder

100g dark chocolate,
chopped

375mL evaporated milk,
chilled

250mL thickened cream,
whipped

1 Combine the egg yolks, sugar, coffee liqueur, coffee powder and dark chocolate in the top of a double saucepan.

2 Stir over simmering water until the chocolate has melted, then cool.

3 Fold in the evaporated milk and cream. Pour into an ice cream machine. Churn until firm and the blades stop turning, approximately 40 minutes. Serve immediately or spoon into a container and freeze.

serves 4

Tiramisu Ice Cream

PREPARATION 2 hrs 45 mins

25g caster sugar

3 tablespoons hot espresso

425g carton ready-to-serve
custard

250g mascarpone cheese

100g cocoa amaretti biscuits,
roughly crumbled

3 tablespoons Marsala

1 Mix the sugar and coffee together and stir until the sugar has dissolved. Whisk together the custard and mascarpone until smooth, then stir in the coffee mixture, mixing evenly.

2 Pour into a freezer container and freeze for 1 hour or until ice crystals begin to form. Whisk the mixture until smooth, then return to the freezer for 30 minutes.

3 Sprinkle the biscuits with the Marsala and quickly stir into the half-frozen ice cream, mixing well. Return to the freezer for 1 hour or until firm. Serve the ice cream decorated with curls of chocolate made with a vegetable peeler.

NOTE All the traditional flavours of tiramisu are fused together in this rich, extravagant ice cream. An ice-cream maker will cut down the freezing time, but it's not essential.

serves 4

Quick Tiramisu

PREPARATION 2 hrs

250mL strong coffee

125mL Tia Maria

250mL thickened cream

250mL mascarpone cheese

75g caster sugar

24 sponge fingers

50g plain chocolate, grated

1 Mix together the coffee and the Tia Maria in a bowl. Set aside.

2 Whip the cream until soft peaks form. Fold in the mascarpone and sugar.

3 Soak the sponge fingers two at a time in the coffee mix. Place in the bottom of a serving glass – you may need to break in half to fit into the glass. Top with some of the cream and mascarpone mix and sprinkle on some of the grated chocolate. Repeat, making two more layers, finishing with the cream and mascarpone mix and grated chocolate.

4 Repeat the process, filling the remaining glasses. Cover with cling film and refrigerate for 2 hours.

makes 24

Mexican Coffee Balls

PREPARATION 20 mins

250g chocolate wafers, crushed

250g ground blanched almonds

40g unsweetened cocoa powder

55g white sugar

2 tablespoons instant coffee powder

80mL coffee liqueur

125mL golden syrup

1 Mix the chocolate wafers with the almonds, cocoa powder and sugar.

2 Dissolve the instant coffee in the coffee liqueur and stir into the crumb mixture with the golden syrup.

3 Shape into 50mm balls and roll in cinnamon sugar. Store in refrigerator.

Coffee Zabayon

PREPARATION 20 mins   COOKING 15 mins

4 egg yolks

2 tablespoons sugar

60mL very strong coffee

125mL coffee cream liqueur

pinch of nutmeg

zest of 1 lemon

1 Beat the egg yolks with the sugar in a bowl until the mix is homogenous.

2 Put the bowl in a bain-marie where the temperature should be about 45–50°C.

3 Keep on beating the mix while adding the coffee, liqueur, nutmeg and lemon zest. Whisk the mix in an electric mixer until it becomes creamy.

4 Pour into warm goblets and decorate with whipped cream and powdered cocoa. This zabayon may also be served with chocolate ice-cream.

serves 4

Coffee Charlotte

PREPARATION 3 hrs 20 mins

100g caramel sugar

1 egg

310mL thickened cream,
  whipped

2 tablespoons instant coffee
  powder, dissolved in

1 tablespoon water

60mL rum

200g lady finger biscuits

1 Beat the sugar and egg until light and fluffy. Fold in the whipped cream and coffee.

2 Combine the rum with 125mL water. Dip the biscuits into the rum mixture, then place in a baking pan. Fill the pan with alternating layers of cream and biscuits, ending up with the biscuits.

3 Put it in the refrigerator for three hours, then remove the charlotte from the baking pan shortly before serving. Dust with cocoa and serve.

Baked Coffee Apples

PREPARATION 20 mins   **COOKING** 30 mins

6 large apples

250g raw sugar

60 walnut pieces

30g butter

450mL strong coffee
 (not espresso)

1 Preheat oven to 180°C. Peel the apples and carefully remove the cores with a core-remover, taking care not to damage the fruit.

2 Mix 80g sugar and the walnuts and use the mixture to fill the apple cores, then top each with a knob of butter.

3 Butter a baking pan and put the apples inside, upright, quite tightly packed.

4 Meanwhile, heat 100g of sugar and the coffee until they are well amalgamated.

5 Cover the apples with this syrup, then put them in the oven and watch the cooking.

6 Frequently collect the juice formed in the bottom of the pan, and pour it again over the top of the apples. When almost baked, put the pan on the flame, sprinkle with the remaining sugar, let it caramelize a little and serve.

NOTE To make baked coffee pears, simply substitute pears for apples.

makes 40 pieces

Coffee and Ginger Almond Bread

PREPARATION 20 mins   COOKING 1 hr 35 mins

115g plain flour

2 teaspoons good quality
  ground coffee

3 egg whites

100g caster sugar

75g unsalted almonds
  or hazelnuts

75g glacé ginger,
  finely diced

1 Preheat oven to 170°C. Lightly spray or brush a 7 x 24cm bar tin with unsaturated oil.

2 Sift together the flour and coffee into a bowl. Place the egg whites in a separate bowl and beat until soft peaks form. Gradually beat in the sugar. Continue beating until the sugar dissolves. Fold in the flour mixture. Fold in the nuts and ginger.

3 Spoon the batter into the prepared tin. Bake for 35 minutes. Stand the tin on a wire rack and cool completely. When cold, remove the bread from the tin. Wrap in aluminium foil. Store in a cool place for 1–3 days – the finished bread will be crisper if you can leave it for 2–3 days.

4 Preheat oven to 120°C. Using a very sharp serrated or electric knife, cut the cooked loaf into wafer-thin slices. Place the slices on ungreased baking trays. Bake for 45–60 minutes or until dry and crisp. Cool on wire racks. Store in an airtight container.

NOTE This recipe is only limited by your imagination. You could use any nut, dried fruit or spice you fancy. For something festive, try cherries, mixed peel and brazil nuts, or for an exotic eastern feel use pistachios, glacé pears and ground cardamom.

Index